D1236982

The 50CAN Guide to Building Advocacy Campaigns

This book belongs to:

_____

The 50CAN Guide to Building Advocacy Campaigns

by Marc Porter Magee, Ph.D.

This book would not be possible without the bravery and commitment of all the advocates, some named here and some not, who have spent their lives working to improve the world around them. We are also deeply grateful to every member of the 50CAN fam, from volunteers to staff to board members, who helped us turn these ideas into action. Last, but not least, we want to thank the tireless leaders who came before us and inspired us to begin our own journey as advocates for a better, more just world.

The 50CAN Guide to Building Advocacy Campaigns
Copyright © 2017 by 50CAN, Inc.

50CAN: The 50-State Campaign for Achievement Now
1625 K Street NW, Suite 400
Washington D.C. 20006

Author
Marc Porter Magee, Ph.D.

Editor
Kathryn Duval

Design
House9 Design

Contributors
Atnre Alleyne, May Amoyaw, Derrell Bradford, Kathryn Duval, Elliot Haspel, Martín Pérez Jr., Michelle Rhee and Vallay Varro.

Library of Congress Control Number 2017952980
Paperback ISBN 9 780999 337189

Let's get to work!

We published the inaugural *50CAN Guide to Building Advocacy Campaigns* in 2015 to inspire more people to get involved in local advocacy. Our aim was to make it easier to build successful campaigns by sharing the system we use as a network.

Thousands of people built their own advocacy campaigns with the help from the first iterations of this book. We used their feedback to help us reimagine our approach for this new edition. We hope you will find that it is more than just a book—it's an interactive guide that you can write in, carry into meetings and refer back to throughout your journey as an advocate.

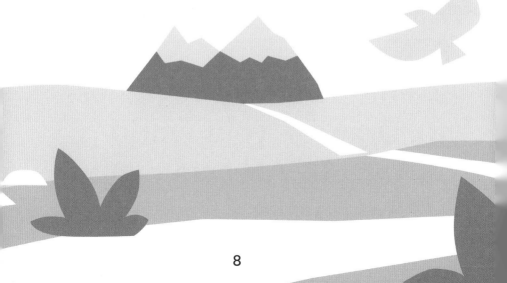

Here is what you need to know:

→ This book is for anyone who is looking for a proven way to build an advocacy campaign, from novices to veterans.

→ Our approach is grounded in the idea of learning by doing. It will guide you through the steps you need to create your own advocacy campaign.

→ It is organized into 11 chapters, each on a different part of your campaign. Each chapter includes instructions, real-life examples, exercises and worksheets.

→ The book also includes a lot of blank spaces to take notes so you can practice in real-time and come back to your ideas.

→ At 50CAN, we use this guidebook to create education advocacy campaigns, but you can use it for a variety of causes that you care about.

→ If you want to join a community of education advocates, we'll tell you how to get involved with our team in the final chapter.

Now more than ever, we need citizen advocates who are working to make the world around them a better, more just place. Are you ready to start your journey? Grab a pencil, turn the page and let's get to work!

Marc Porter Magee
CEO and Founder
@marcportermagee

Vallay Varro
President
@vallay

Derrell Bradford
Executive VP
@dyrnwyn

Chapter 1

The big wide world of advocacy

What is advocacy? Often times, the barrier to getting started in this work begins with the word "advocacy" itself.

The dictionary definition goes something like this: **Advocacy** is a process that people or groups use to advance a cause by influencing decisions within political, economic and social systems.

At 50CAN we prefer environmentalist Aidan Ricketts' description of advocates as "the immune system of the body politic." What that means to us is that advocacy is both natural and necessary in a democracy. We will always have ways that we are falling short as a society. Advocates help us respond to those problems with concrete solutions. They are a critical part of a healthy, living community that is always changing for the better in response to people's needs.

Most advocacy efforts are organized into **campaigns:** efforts designed to achieve a clear goal in a specific amount of time. Advocacy is most effective when it has a beginning, middle and end.

Your turn! What does advocacy mean to you?
Write down what comes to mind:

Who can build an advocacy campaign?

As you work your way through this book, you'll hear from advocates themselves about the work they have done and the campaigns they have built. Some advocates are professionals. Some are parents working on their ideas part-time. Some are community leaders inspired to do more for their neighbors.

What all advocates have in common is their belief that tomorrow can be better than today. They believe they can play a role in ways big and small to help us get to a better tomorrow. When you set your mind to making a difference, and then get to work on that idea, you become an advocate.

Who is an advocate you admire in your life? Write down their name along with a few ways they are making a difference.

Advocate's name:

The way(s) they are making a difference:

Where can you build an advocacy campaign?

Advocacy campaigns can be built anywhere and come in all shapes and sizes. Some take place in a neighborhood and last for a few weeks. Others take place across a whole nation and may go on for years or decades before achieving their goals. Change is possible across a wide variety of geographies. What we've learned at 50CAN is that one of the best places to start an advocacy campaign is in your own backyard.

Take a look at where 50CAN supports advocacy campaigns across the country:

What advocacy campaigns are happening right now that are inspiring you? Where are they taking place? Write down a few examples below.

Key definitions
from this chapter

Advocacy → the natural and necessary process within a democracy of responding to problems with concrete solutions (organized into campaigns) to achieve a clear goal in a specific amount of time

My notes from this chapter

Chapter 2

The three steps to building an advocacy campaign

What makes great advocates is the discipline they bring to this complex work. They know the one key to maximizing their odds of success: don't skip steps!

The best way to avoid skipping steps is to follow a plan. In this chapter you will learn the three-step approach we use for building campaigns at 50CAN:

① Clarify goals,

② Match strategy to the environment, and

③ Select winning tactics.

Once you commit to not skipping steps, it's amazing how many times you catch yourself and others talking tactics first. It's easy to jump right into tactics because they are so concrete and connected to action. But doing before thinking makes it less likely that you will be successful in your advocacy. It also runs the risk of an end result that doesn't make you happy.

Climbing to the summit

One way to think about these steps is
to imagine yourself climbing a mountain.
What will it take to make it to the top?

① Clarify goals

While your vision is to climb a mountain, your goal is the specific destination on the mountain that you are trying to reach. Now, take out your binoculars and explore the peaks. Where do you want to finish your climb? You need to know where you want to plant your flag before you take your first step.

On the mountain on the right, **draw a flag** on the peak where you will finish your climb. That is the goal of your campaign.

② Match strategy to environment

Think of strategies as the different paths you might take to the top. Some might be well-worn paths around the side of the mountain. Some might be shorter paths with steeper slopes. Take time to study the options because the path you choose is one of the most important decisions you will make.

Look carefully at the four paths up the mountain. Choose the path you would take. Now **connect the path you have chosen to your flag**.

③ Select winning tactics

Tactics are the steps you take to move forward on your chosen path. The number of steps will depend on the type of journey you chose. Those steps become the actions that get you where you want to go.

How many steps will it take to reach your goal? **Draw five to 10 footprints** along your path up the mountain.

19

Marc's race to the top

Hi! I'm Marc Porter Magee. In 2009, I was working on an education advocacy campaign in Connecticut when we heard of a federal education competition called Race to the Top. The more we talked with our supporters, the more we realized what a big opportunity this competition could be. We decided to drop our original campaign goal for the year. In its place, we drafted a plan to run an advocacy campaign that could help Connecticut win this competition. We focused on securing four key policy changes in the upcoming legislative session:

→ Performance-based teacher evaluations
→ Alternative pathways to becoming a principal
→ More rigorous standards
→ Support for charter school growth

It quickly became clear how hard this would be. Connecticut's commissioner of education said the state didn't need any policy changes to win the competition. We developed a two-part plan to build support behind our reforms. First, we would engage in elite negotiations. However, in order to do that we needed to master the details of the Race to the Top rules. It also meant sharing what it would take to win with key policymakers. Second, we would initiate a social movement effort by organizing parents, teachers and concerned citizens as voices for change.

The first step we took in the campaign was policy analysis. We broke down the complex Race to the Top scoring system to understand what it would take to win. This analysis helped us demonstrate how our four policy changes would increase the odds of success. It also helped us secure media hits that discussed how the state's initial application had fallen short.

While these initial steps were helpful, we knew that they wouldn't be enough. The reforms in our campaign were significant and would require a major show of public support. During the course of the campaign, we kept in touch with our supporters through short video updates. With a few weeks left in the legislative session, we asked supporters to testify at a critical legislative hearing for the bills. The call to action was answered by more than 500 people who showed up at the statehouse.

In the end, the bills passed and the four policy changes were signed into law. The 2009–10 legislative session ended up being one of the state's busiest and most successful.

Before we look at each step in the campaign planning process, try your hand at identifying the goals, strategies and tactics from Marc's story. Don't worry if you run into trouble! By the end of chapter five, we will have explored each step in depth.

What were the goals of this campaign?

① _____

② _____

③ _____

④ _____

What were the strategies?

① _____

② _____

What were the tactics?

① _____

② _____

③ _____

④ _____

Check your answers against the key below. How did you do? What was the easiest element of the campaign to identify? What was the hardest?

21

Keep an eye on the weather

Building a strong, focused plan is key to being an effective advocate. But it's also important to know when to be flexible.

Imagine you are back in the valley looking up at the mountain. You know where you want to plant your flag. You've chosen a path to the top. You've thought about the steps you want to take. But then, right before you are about to leave, a storm blows in. Should you wait a few days before you set off, or should you stick to your schedule? Perhaps you need to reevaluate the route you were planning to take, or which peak you had chosen as your destination.

Take another look at the story about Race to the Top. Our team was planning on a campaign with a different goal. But the winds shifted and a new opportunity emerged. We changed the destination of our plan to take advantage of these new conditions, and that made all the difference.

Be specific about your destination

Your advocacy journey won't always be easy. One thing that can help ensure you are successful is clearly defining what a win looks like before you start.

When climbing a mountain you want to be clear about how close to the summit you need to get to make the climb worth it. In an advocacy campaign you want to be able to answer specific questions about your destination. Which parts of your goals are the most important? What needs to be in place for you to make a difference? Where could you compromise?

If you write down answers to these questions before you begin, you increase the odds of a successful journey.

Key definitions from this chapter

Goals → what you hope to achieve with your advocacy campaign

Strategies → the path you travel to reach your goal

Tactics → the action steps you take along your path in pursuit of your goal

My notes from this chapter

"I alone cannot change the world, but I can cast a stone
across the waters to create many ripples."
—Saint Teresa of Calcutta, advocate for the poor

Chapter 3

Clarify goals

There is nothing worse than "winning" your campaign and then finding out that the changes you secured don't solve the problem. That's why it is so important to develop a clear destination before you start your advocacy journey. You can use the process outlined below to clarify your goals and help ensure this doesn't happen to you. We will go deeper into each step in this chapter.

① **Start with values**
Be prepared to share your story. What are the life experiences that brought you to this cause? What issues are you most passionate about? Why are you compelled to advocate for these issues?

② **Listen and learn**
The best advocates are great listeners. What don't you know that others could teach you? Who can help you broaden your thinking? Who in your community is touched by the issue you are working on? We have found that before choosing your goals, it is best to go on a listening tour.

③ **Craft a vision**
The only way you can be sure that you are headed toward the right destination is to get your plan down on paper. How will the world be better if you are successful in your campaign?

Elliot's core values

Hi! I'm Elliot Haspel. Sometimes your own advocacy is grounded in adversity. When I was in sixth grade, I slipped while running through the playground and knocked my head into a metal slide. What my doctors didn't understand at the time was that the accident had damaged my brain's ability to regulate emotions. In the middle of class, I would sometimes fly into a rage when little things went wrong. I was not able to attend a full week's worth of school for two years.

But I was lucky. For the next several years, every adult in my life—my parents, teachers, principal, doctors and counselors—leaned in. They poured extra time and energy into creating an environment where my learning could continue. I got to work rebuilding the impulse controls that the accident had taken away.

When I became a fourth-grade teacher, I began to realize just how unusual my network of support had been. Many students in my class were struggling with their own traumas, physical and otherwise. Rather than getting the support they needed, they were labeled or ignored. The system was failing brilliant kids every day.

The three **core values** I took from my experiences—empathy, understanding and dedication—serve as the moral foundation for my advocacy work today.

Your turn! Elliot's advocacy is driven forward by his own experiences as a student and teacher. What compels you to be an advocate? What values will drive your campaign?

27

Atnre's listening tour

Hi! I'm Atnre Alleyne. My mother gave me the ancient Egyptian name Atnreakn, raised me in the world of civil rights and sent me to high school in Ghana because she believed in countering the assertions of the inferiority of people of African descent. The picture below is one of my most treasured possessions—a photo of myself as a young boy at home with civil rights leader Stokely Carmichael, who famously said: "organize, organize, organize."

While leading research efforts on teacher effectiveness at the Delaware Department of Education, I saw first-hand how students and families weren't in the room to influence key decisions. I spent a year traveling around my state in the hopes of building a grassroots advocacy campaign. I met with nearly 600 parents, students, teachers and concerned citizens to find out what it would take to build an education system that does not treat large groups of students as inferior and unworthy of a high-quality education.

Through this **listening tour** I developed a new advocacy organization with a policy agenda grounded in the hopes and dreams of the students and families I met along the way.

Your turn! Atnre's advocacy is grounded in his belief that a great education starts with empowered students and families. What kind of change do you want to achieve in your community? Who do you need to hear from to ensure the people you want to serve are truly represented in your work?

Want to embark on a listening tour of your own? Use the **Listening tour questionnaire** in the back of the book to help structure your conversations.

Crafting a vision with change lenses

Improving your world is easier when you ground your thinking in how things get better over time. We have found that it helps to stretch your mind by thinking about change through different lenses. When you see how the world looks through these different perspectives, you form a more complete picture of the best way to reach your goal. Through 50CAN's hundreds of campaigns we have found four change lenses that help advocates choose smarter goals.

Community
Effective, sustainable policy change requires strong relationships, real-time feedback and long-term ownership by the people served.

Competition
Greater responsiveness and better outcomes are more likely when people have the power to choose among multiple options to meet their needs.

Performance
Success requires both the flexibility to pursue excellence and rigorous standards to ensure those serving the public are held accountable for their results.

Pluralism
Diverse populations are better served by dynamic systems that support lots of paths to success and embrace different traditions, values and beliefs.

Turning around a low-performing school district

The best way to understand how these change lenses can broaden your thinking is to look at an actual case study: turning around a low-performing school district. Imagine you are a new superintendent hired to turn around a low-performing district. Read the four perspectives below and think about how your actions might be different depending on how you are looking at the opportunity for change.

Community
No one cares more about a child's success than his or her family. By giving parents and families more of a voice over school changes, you can create the deep community support needed for sustainable change.

Competiton
There is power in helping people vote with their feet. By offering families choices between different types of schools, you can create stronger incentives for everyone in your school system to be more responsive to the needs of students and their families.

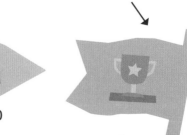

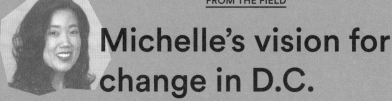

Michelle's vision for change in D.C.

Hi! I'm Michelle Rhee. My career in education has included being a third-grade classroom teacher, a nonprofit leader for teacher recruitment and the honor of being the Chancellor of District of Columbia Public Schools. When I stepped into the role of chancellor, the D.C. school district was one of the lowest-performing districts in the country. I had some hard choices to make about what kind of changes would ensure that students got the education they deserved.

I decided to focus on **performance** by setting higher standards for our schools, using regular assessments to understand how well students were doing, closing down schools that were regularly failing students and rewarding teachers for the growth their students made during the year. Over the decade that followed, the enrollment decline in D.C. public schools reversed and students in the district saw greater gains on the National Assessment of Educational Progress than students in any of the 50 states.

In reflecting on my time in D.C., I've realized that viewing these changes through a performance lens was only part of the picture. In hindsight, our district reform efforts benefited from the **competitive** pressure from the public charter and private school sectors.

At the same time, our investments in new schools should have taken **pluralism** more strongly into account to include many different models of school success.

Most importantly, using a **community** lens earlier on in my planning would have helped me see the ways parents and families can be given real ownership over these change efforts. In my work as an advocate, I still aim to make performance a key part of the solution but also use the additional lenses to get the full picture of sustainable education reform.

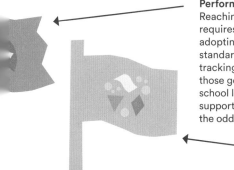

Performance
Reaching excellence requires aiming high. By adopting more rigorous standards, regularly tracking progress towards those goals and giving your school leaders flexibility and support, you can increase the odds of success.

Pluralism
In education, one size doesn't fit all. To help ensure students find their way to an educational environment where they can thrive, you can partner with local civic groups to create a greater variety of educational paths to success.

Test your knowledge!

How well do you know the four change lenses? Find out by reading the six real-life examples below and then matching each goal to the correct change lens.

Harlem Children's Zone
This effort aims to break the cycle of generational poverty. It focuses on creating strong relationships with parents, families and children living in 100 blocks of Harlem and providing them with long-term support through comprehensive parenting, health and educational services.

Faith-based initiative
This effort aims to strengthen America's social support services by embracing the work of a wide variety of different religious groups. Using approaches grounded in their traditions and values, faith-based groups work on issues from combatting homelessness to helping people recover from addiction.

SpaceX
This corporation is part of a new push to create private alternatives to the government-run space agencies that have traditionally held a monopoly on launching spacecraft. SpaceX aims to revolutionize spaceflight by providing the choice of cheaper, reusable rockets.

Emissions trading
This initiative, also called "cap and trade," is a market-based approach to controlling pollution using choices rather than mandates. It gives private-sector companies incentives to reduce their pollution and sell their pollution credits through a marketplace.

School accountability system
This approach focuses on creating a uniform system for reporting on how schools are performing using a common set of standards. It helps education officials hold schools publicly accountable for results.

Community policing
This effort encourages police to build deep relationships in communities. These officers have a long-term commitment to specific neighborhoods. They walk the beat every day, building trust and ensuring real-time feedback from the people they serve.

Connect each initiative to its corresponding change lens

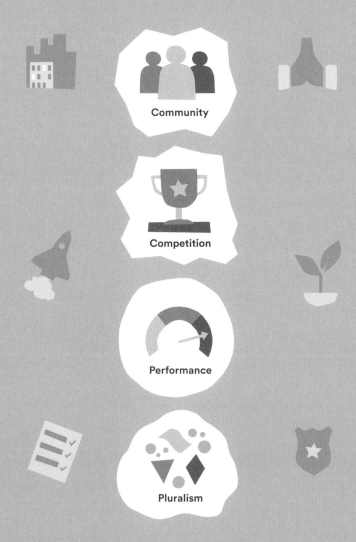

Community

Competition

Performance

Pluralism

Clarify your goal with change lenses

How can you use the four change lenses to stretch your thinking about your goals? Take a moment to write down in a sentence or two the goal of your advocacy campaign. Then use the checklist on the right to assess your approach against the four change lenses. Are there ways you can clarify your goal so that it is stronger across all four change lenses?

The goal of my advocacy campaign is to:

After you have filled out the checked boxes on the right, are there any ways you might adapt your goal to better account for these four perspectives?

The change lens checklist

Community

○ Builds strong relationships with people served

○ Draws upon a deep understanding of the local context

○ Gives the community ownership of decisions

Competition

☐ Allows multiple providers to vie for users

☐ Provides high-quality information to users

☐ Gives providers incentives for improvement and success

Performance

◇ Empowers strong leaders to make decisions

◇ Sets rigorous standards for success

◇ Holds parties accountable for results

Pluralism

⬡ Allows for multiple, unique pathways to success

⬡ Encourages all groups to join

⬡ Embraces diversity and differences

Key definitions from this chapter

Listening tour → the activity of meeting with people who will be affected by your goal in order to record their viewpoints and create buy-in for your work

Community → a change lens where effective, sustainable policy change requires strong relationships, real-time feedback and long-term ownership by the people served

Competition → a change lens where empowered people choose among multiple options to meet their needs, thereby ensuring greater responsiveness and driving better outcomes

Performance → a change lens where success requires both the flexibility to pursue excellence and rigorous standards to ensure those serving the public are held accountable for their results

Pluralism → a change lens where a dynamic system supports lots of paths to success and embraces different traditions, values and beliefs to better serve a diverse population

My notes from this chapter

"Every great dream begins with a dreamer. Always remember,
you have within you the strength, the patience and the passion
to reach for the stars to change the world."
—Harriet Tubman, anti-slavery advocate

Chapter 4

Match strategy to environment

After decades of research examining thousands of advocacy campaigns across hundreds of issues, political scientists have found that a few key strategies regularly get results. Like most things in life, the more thought you put into choosing a strategy, the more successful you will be.

Four strategies for success

Elite negotiation
Advocates work to influence people who already hold power. By tapping into the interests of public officials, this approach secures change through trading and compromise.

Social movements
A large number of people build their power to secure change by organizing around common goals. By operating outside of the existing system, this approach can change the status quo in profound ways.

Expert communities
Trusted people with knowledge on a particular subject change the public debate by reaching consensus. By translating consensus into advice on solutions, they influence policy and practice.

Emergent networks
People use trial and error to discover solutions to a problem. By testing and refining their approach over time, they develop proof points for widespread change.

Multiple paths to a community garden

The best way to understand the four strategies for success is to see them in action. Below we explore how each pathway might be used for a common goal: providing school children with access to community gardens. Read the four approaches below and then read May's story on the path she chose.

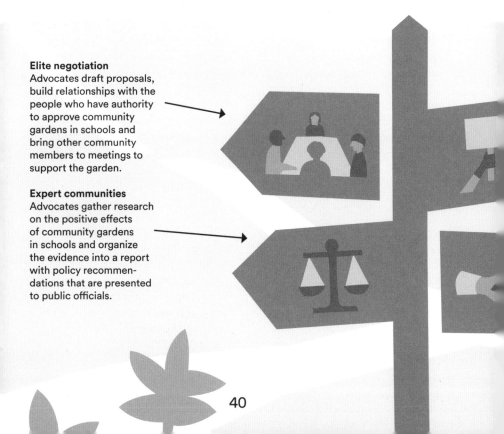

Elite negotiation
Advocates draft proposals, build relationships with the people who have authority to approve community gardens in schools and bring other community members to meetings to support the garden.

Expert communities
Advocates gather research on the positive effects of community gardens in schools and organize the evidence into a report with policy recommendations that are presented to public officials.

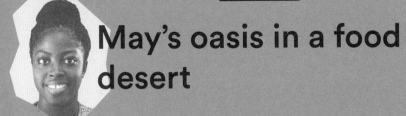

May's oasis in a food desert

Hi! I'm May Amoyaw and I'm a first-grade teacher in Baltimore, Maryland. I saw first-hand the problems my students faced every day because they were stuck in a food desert. I wanted to empower students to take responsibility for their own communities and to live healthy lives.

My idea was that every school could have fresh produce that is grown by the students themselves. After exploring all four advocacy strategies, I decided on the **emergent networks** pathway to my goal.

First I raised a small amount of money from friends, family and neighbors. I then partnered with a local recreation center to make room for student gardens. I also worked with a farmers' market to allow the students to sell what they grew.

The project proved that we can teach children the importance of healthy eating habits, give them an opportunity to run a small business and provide fresh food options for their community. It was so successful that the program is now being adapted for schools all across Baltimore!

Social movements
Advocates reach out to gardening clubs around the city to recruit members to their cause, culminating in a public rally to support the community gardens initiative.

Emergent networks
Advocates partner with schools to test out the idea of a community garden. The lessons learned from this work inform a new local policy.

Test your knowledge!

How well do you know the four advocacy strategies? Find out by reading the six advocacy examples below. Then match them to the correct advocacy strategy on the right.

The Affordable Care Act

This effort was supported by an enormous lobbying effort, backed by stakeholder groups like the American Medical Association with significant political clout. They created an incentive among policymakers to draft a compromise bill that could secure the necessary votes to pass.

Personalized learning

This effort encourages teachers and administrators to discover new solutions to ensure that all students can learn in a way that works for them. It aims to connect innovative educators together so they can combine their best practices to shape education policy.

Marriage equality

This effort centered on an emotional call to action from advocacy groups who organized their supporters into a powerful force for change. These many voices were focused on a single goal that upended the status quo.

Global warming

This effort is focused on organizing the results of complex research and analysis into trustworthy policy conclusions. The goal is broad consensus among experts about the problem, its causes and potential solutions.

Women's suffrage

This effort was driven forward by compelling spokespeople who rallied mass support around the right of women to vote. The work was driven forward through large marches and protests that operated outside of traditional political forums.

Americans with Disabilities Act

This effort resulted in a federal law that provides civil rights protections to people with disabilities. It was the result of an intense lobbying effort by advocacy groups and the bipartisan leadership of influential senators.

Connect each advocacy campaign to its strategy

Elite Negotiation

Social movements

Expert communities

Emergent networks

Choosing the right strategies

Which advocacy strategies should you use in your campaign? Take a moment to review the strategy checklist on the right. Think about which success factors are in place right now or could be put in place with a little work. Then fill in the check boxes that apply to your campaign.

After you have filled out your checklist, add up the number of checked boxes under each strategy. Write down the strategies below in order from the one with the most success factors to the least:

① ....

② ....

③ ....

④ ....

You can increase your odds of reaching the summit by exploring different paths to your goal. Draw stars next to the two strategies that seem most promising to you—we'll come back to them later.

The strategy checklist

Elite negotiation

- ◯ An urgent public problem of interest to policymakers
- ◯ Easily understood and credible options to act on
- ◯ Incentives for legislators to make change

Social movements

- ◇ A clear call to action
- ◇ Compelling spokespeople who can dramatize the injustice
- ◇ Well-organized supporters and advocates

Expert communities

- ☐ A well-defined but complex public policy problem
- ☐ Expert agreement on the problem, causes and possible solutions
- ☐ Policymaker interest in expert guidance

Emergent networks

- ⬡ Well-defined areas of innovative practice related to the problem
- ⬡ Incentives for innovators to join together
- ⬡ Policymaker interest in translating practice into policy

Key definitions
from this chapter

Elite negotiation → a strategy where advocates work to influence people who already hold power

Social movements → a strategy where a large number of people build their power to secure change by organizing around common goals

Expert communities → a strategy where trusted people with knowledge on a particular subject change the public debate by reaching consensus

Emergent networks → a strategy where people working on a problem discover new solutions through trial and error and develop proof points for widespread change

My notes from this chapter

"Not everything that is faced can be changed, but
nothing can be changed until it is faced."
—James Baldwin, civil rights advocate

Chapter 5

Select winning tactics

If picking the right strategy is like choosing the path toward your destination, tactics are the steps you take along your journey. Advocacy tactics must be paired thoughtfully with your strategy to ensure you make it all the way to the summit. Just like in the last chapter, the more you practice, the better you get. The first step in mastering tactics is to be able to recognize them in a real-world advocacy campaign.

FROM THE FIELD

Vallay's push for pre-K

Hi! My name is Vallay Varro. I've been working in education for my entire adult life.

My first advocacy campaign was in Minnesota and focused on new ways to bring a high-quality education to all kids in my state. I began with a listening tour to connect with other families about their education priorities. I was struck by how often the need for quality preschool was brought up by parents. My research confirmed what I was hearing from parents: Only 1.5 percent of Minnesota three- and four-year-olds were enrolled in state-funded preschool programs, one-tenth the national average.

In our first campaign, we lobbied the governor and the legislature with the facts about the positive impact of expanding quality preschool. Yet almost out of nowhere the whole effort was derailed by a small group who were against our plan's quality rating system. It was time for Plan B.

Over the next 36 hours we organized an open letter to the governor urging him to do everything in his power to ensure the program became a reality. More than 40 community leaders and local policymakers signed the letter. But with time running out, we knew we needed to do more. We got to work on a clear call to action for the governor to implement the program by executive order.

We decided to use a powerful visual metaphor to make the point that the state was blindfolding parents and keeping them from making informed choices. I sent an email to our growing group of supporters with a simple request: join me by sending in a photo with a blindfold over your eyes. Over the next few days, photos poured in from parents across the state. To make sure these photos weren't ignored, we designed an advertising campaign that ran around the clock on a news site frequented by Minnesota lawmakers. In a final push, we made a photo book of all the participants and hand-delivered it to the governor's office.

In the end we not only secured $4 million to get the new program off the ground but also succeeded in getting the governor to expand the accountability system statewide.

Circle the tactics Vallay used in her campaign. Write down the three you think made the greatest difference below.

① _____

② _____

③ _____

Getting to work!
While there are hundreds of different tactics in the world of advocacy, there are a few top tactics that we come back to time and again. If you can master these basic tactics, you will be well on your way to carrying out campaign strategies in service of a wide variety of goals.

Of course, by choosing your strategy first, you give yourself an additional advantage because different strategies lend themselves to a different set of tactics. On the right are the most common tactics used in advocacy campaigns, sorted by the four strategies introduced in the last chapter.

Which tactics are you most comfortable with right now? Check those boxes. Which tactics are you most interested in learning how to use? Underline those. Do you see any patterns?

Take a moment to write down the tactics you think might be most useful in your campaign:

_____

_____

Top tactics for each strategy

Elite negotiation

- ◯ Lobbying
- ◯ Power mapping
- ◯ Negotiation
- ◯ Policy analysis
- ◯ Bill drafting
- ◯ Coalition building
- ◯ Media relations
- ◯ Campaign donations

Expert communities

- ☐ Research studies and reports
- ☐ Legal action
- ☐ Conferences
- ☐ Public debates
- ☐ Advisory groups
- ☐ Policy proposals
- ☐ Letters to the editor
- ☐ Legislative testimony

Social movements

- ◇ Grassroots organizing
- ◇ Training spokespeople
- ◇ Marches
- ◇ Boycotts
- ◇ Sit-ins and occupations
- ◇ Storytelling
- ◇ Petition drives
- ◇ Door knocking

Emergent networks

- ⬡ Experimentation
- ⬡ Field visits
- ⬡ Peer networking
- ⬡ Toolkits
- ⬡ Newsletters
- ⬡ Trainings
- ⬡ Success stories
- ⬡ Social media campaigns

My notes from this chapter

"I am fundamentally an optimist. Part of being an optimist is keeping one's head pointed toward the sun, one's feet moving forward."
—Nelson Mandela, anti-apartheid advocate

Chapter 6

Storytelling

Storytelling is something we all do in our daily lives. Whether you're holding court at a party with a dramatic description of your day or explaining something to a colleague with an example from your life, you are practicing storytelling more often than you think. So how can you use this tactic effectively in advocacy?

The who, the what and the why now
Some stories are told better than others. The secret to developing a powerful story is to make sure it answers three key questions:

① Who?

Does this issue touch you or someone you love? Let your listener into your world. Share something about the person you do this work for, whether it's yourself, a family member, a friend or a neighbor.

② What?

What are you trying to accomplish? What will need to change? What happens if your work is successful? What happens if it is not?

③ Why now?

It's easy for life to get in the way of a cause. Why do people need to make time for this cause right now? Be specific in explaining the urgency. When you tell someone your "why now," it equips them with the reason to stop what they are doing and get involved.

Strive for simplicity
The world of advocacy is complex but your reason for doing the work doesn't have to be. When telling your story, keep it simple. Tell people why you are doing your work in clear terms rooted in your own experience.

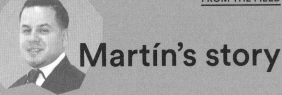

Martín's story

Hi! I'm Martín Pérez Jr. I got my start in education as a classroom teacher, but my story begins in Compton, California, where I grew up.

My parents loved my brother and me very much but they struggled to give us everything they knew we needed. They were only able to save up enough money to send one of us to a Jesuit high school. They chose me. **My brother** had to stay behind in the district high school we were assigned to.

Four years later, I became the first person in my family to be accepted into college. That same week my brother was convicted of a crime and sent to Los Angeles County jail. Four years after that, I walked across the stage as a graduate of University of California, Berkeley, and my brother was entering the penitentiary system for the second time. My brother and I had the same parents and the same potential. But there was one thing that we did not have in common: the same educational opportunities.

I know that opportunity gap is what made our lives as different as they are, and that knowledge has left a scar on my heart. I went to college to become the teacher my brother never had—the one who would understand him and take the time to connect with him. The one who he would remember later in life, thinking, "If not for this teacher, I would be in jail."

The difficult truth is that my path diverged from my brother's so dramatically because **we ration high-quality education** in our country. There just aren't enough good schools to go around. It's students from low-income families—like my brother—who pay the price with their freedom. The research and statistics show us this is true, but it is also my life. I live with that difficult truth every day. It opened my eyes in a way that means they will never be closed.

That's why I'm an advocate for changing the way our school system works. We need to open as many high-quality schools as are needed to make sure everyone gets the opportunity they deserve. **Somewhere right now there is a kid like my brother.** He is stuck in a failing school. We still have time to reach him—but time is running out.

Tell your story, one step at a time

Go back to page 34 where you wrote down your advocacy goal. Think about the story you want to tell about why you're doing this work. Then answer the three questions below. Want to practice telling a few different stories? There are extra copies of this worksheet in the back of the guidebook.

Who do you know who is touched by this issue?

What needs to change?

Why does it need to happen now?

Pull it together into one short story below:

Now it's time to practice! Find opportunities to tell your story over and over again: in the car, in the shower, on a walk, to friends, to strangers, to anyone who will listen. The more you tell your story, the more effective your storytelling skills will become.

My notes from this chapter

"Once social change begins, it cannot be reversed.
You cannot un-educate the person who has learned to read."
—César Chávez, labor advocate

Chapter 7

Power
mapping

Power mapping is a tactic you can use to find the people who will help you in your campaign. It's also a way to identify the chain of relationships that will help you influence them.

① Map the landscape

The first step in power mapping is to draw the world through the eyes of the goal you are trying to achieve. Brainstorm the people who could have a role in your successes and failures. Rank these people according to how supportive they are of your goal and how influential they will be in helping you achieve it.

② Choose your targets

Your top targets will be the people most likely to be able to emerge as strong champions of your goal. Often they will be people you have ranked as both supportive and influential. Sometimes they won't start out as strong supporters initially. Instead you will have to persuade them.

③ Identify their influencers

It can be difficult to influence top targets directly, so the next step is to get to know the people who can influence them. Using the power map diagram, map out the names of people in different spheres of influence around the decision maker: family members, friends, business partners.

④ Make a plan

Using your power map as a guide, choose the top influencers you want to connect with. Then get to work finding ways to reach out to them and get them on your side. Consider using a storytelling tactic (like in the last chapter) to make the most of your time with them.

Mapping a city

Let's look at how power mapping works in action. Below is a landscape analysis and a power map for a campaign to promote a greater investment in after-school programming in a city. After mapping out the landscape, our advocate has chosen the mayor as the best target on the issue. She then got to work mapping out who might be able to help secure a meeting with the mayor to ask him to endorse the idea.

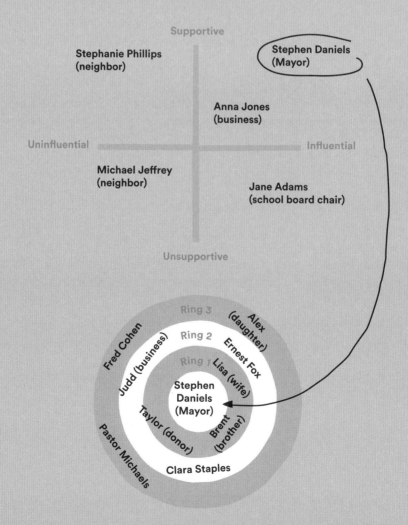

Your turn! Don't worry if you don't have all the information you need right now. Just jump in and start to get a feel for using this tactic in your campaign. Start by brainstorming all the different people in your world. Rate them in terms of support and influence. Then circle the name of the person with the best mix of influence and support. Last but not least, brainstorm the people who are connected to this decision maker. Need more paper? There are extra copies of these worksheets in the back of the guidebook!

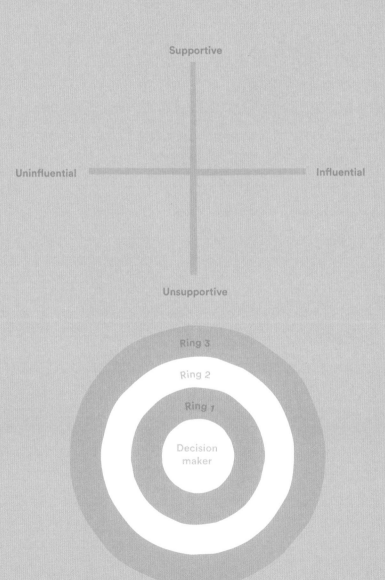

Key definitions
from this chapter

Power mapping → a tool to find the people who will help you in your campaign and identify ways to reach them
Landscape analysis → the first step in power mapping which lists out the people involved in your work and their level of support and influence on your goal

My notes from this chapter

"There may be times when we are powerless to prevent injustice,
but there must never be a time when we fail to protest."
—Elie Wiesel, human rights advocate

Chapter 8

Negotiation

Negotiation is a tactic that people use to try and resolve their differences and reach a mutually beneficial outcome. It's also the main way most public policy debates are decided. Negotiations often end in compromise, but that doesn't mean that each group has given up equal amounts of what they wanted. Knowing how to negotiate for your cause will help ensure the deal you reach makes a difference.

Start with no. Don't begin by trying to think up win-win scenarios that will ensure a deal is reached. Instead, start by thinking about what specifically would make a good deal for you. Before negotiating you should be clear where you will draw the line and say no. Write down what those specific points are so they don't get lost in the heat of the back and forth. Make sure to do your homework on what kind of changes are needed to make a difference. That way, when you say no, you say it with confidence and conviction that is grounded in the needs of your cause.

Strengthen your BATNA. BATNA stands for "Best Alternative To a Negotiated Agreement." It's what you turn to if your negotiation fails. If you are trying to buy a car, your BATNA is the price the next dealership will give you. You are much better off if you know the price the second dealership will offer before you start negotiating with the first. The best way to strengthen your BATNA is to develop it before the negotiations are underway. This will help increase your leverage to get a better deal in the negotiations. It will also help you avoid the mistake of walking away from a compromise that is better than your next best alternative.

Build a three-sided box. You often hear advocates say that they are trying to "box people in." That's not really the goal. We want things to change, not keep people in place where they are. So while working to strengthen your next best alternative, you also want to consider ways to increase pressure on the other side to compromise. The reason the box has three sides and not four is that you want to allow the person to be able to embrace the compromise and be celebrated for it. That is the ultimate win-win in advocacy.

Derrell's New Jersey negotiation

Hi! I'm Derrell Bradford. I've been an education advocate for fifteen years and I got my start in a series of campaigns to improve educational opportunities in New Jersey. I've found myself turning to negotiation time and again when working to get meaningful changes for kids. A few years ago I was part of a campaign to ensure every child in the state was taught by a great teacher. The political winds were in our favor because the governor made it clear that this was one of his top priorities, so it fell to us to negotiate a win.

Starting with no. Step one was to figure out what would have to be included in any deal to make sure that it actually helped kids. The governor had recently implemented a new statewide teacher evaluation system. So what we needed was a law that would tie teacher tenure to effectiveness to make the system work. We were prepared to walk away from any compromise that didn't accomplish that goal.

Strengthening our BATNA. Our plan was to work with our supporters in the Senate to draft a strong bill. Then we would put pressure on the Assembly to ensure that it reached the governor's desk. Our "Best Alternative to a Negotiated Agreement" was either a lawsuit to potentially force the change or an effort to elect new representatives who would be more supportive. The problem with a lawsuit was that it could take years. The problem with a political route was that it would be very expensive and might backfire.

Building a three-sided box. We got to work building pressure on the Assembly to act. One side of the box was an advertising campaign on the urgency of these changes. We also worked with the media to explain why our tenure law—the oldest in the country—was holding our schools back. Lastly, we kept up an intensive lobbying effort at the capitol.

In the end, a law was passed that tied tenure to effectiveness. It didn't accomplish everything we wanted but it helped us achieve our ultimate goal. The bill, TEACH NJ, passed the state legislature with a unanimous vote.

Your turn! Use the template below to draft the BATNA for your campaign. Start by writing down the goal you're working on. Then think about what your agreement absolutely must have in it to be something you would agree to. Lastly, think about how else you might achieve this goal if negotiations fail and what you are likely to achieve through that approach. Don't worry, there are extra copies of the worksheet at the end of the guidebook if you'd like to try this again!

Negotiation worksheet

Goal

A negotiated agreement must include...

Best alternative to a negotiated agreement (BATNA)

1.

2.

3.

Key definitions from this chapter

Negotiation → the process people undertake to try and resolve their differences and reach a mutually beneficial outcome
BATNA → Best Alternative To a Negotiated Agreement

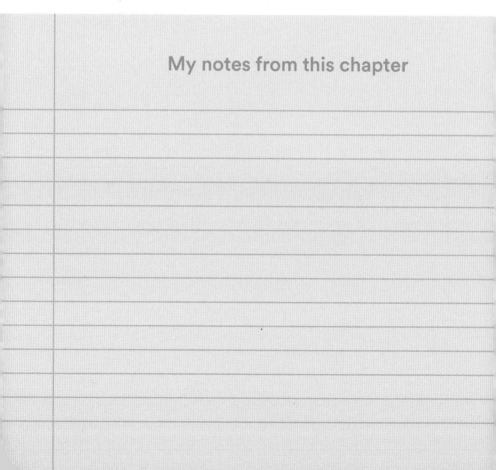

My notes from this chapter

Chapter 9

Put the pieces together

It might not feel like it now, but your campaign plan is almost finished! All you need to do is put the pieces together in one place.

Building your plan

① Goal

Flip back to page 34 and find the place where you wrote down your goal. Is there anything you want to change based on what you've learned? Take a moment to refine the wording and then write down your goal in the box in the template.

② Strategy

Go to page 44. Review the ranked list of strategies you wrote down. Which two strategies do you think will be most helpful in achieving your goals? Write them down in the strategy boxes below your goal.

③ Tactics

Go to page 50. Review the list of tactics you originally wrote down. How do they look? Are there any you would take off? Any you want to add? Review which tactics match up to the two strategies you have selected. Write down the tactics you want to use in your campaign.

④ Define a win

Go to page 67 where you thought about what a win would look like to you. Write a short sentence in the box on the next page about what needs to be in place to declare victory.

⑤ Obstacles

One last thing! Remember to keep an eye on the obstacles in your path. Go to page 22 and think about what could get in the way of you reaching your destination. Write down those potential obstacles in the obstacles box.

The first draft of campaign planning is always the hardest. As you begin to carry out your plan, you may find that some things need to change—that's okay. We've included additional blank campaign planning templates at the end of the guidebook. You can use those to adapt and evolve your plan.

My campaign plan

Goal

Strategy #1	Strategy #2

Tactics linked to strategy	Tactics linked to strategy
1.	1.
2.	2.
3.	3.

A win looks like:

Potential obstacles:

Don't forget to celebrate your success along the way!

When climbing a mountain, it is important to leave time to catch your breath and appreciate the progress you have made. There is nothing like taking in the view of the valley below to give you the energy you need to reach the summit. The same is true in advocacy. Make time during your journey to appreciate how much you have accomplished since you started. Reflect on what you have learned along the way. Celebrate when you reach important milestones.

My notes from this chapter

"Democracy is not just a set of institutions or rules,
it is a daily cultural practice."
—Aidan Ricketts, environmental advocate

My notes from this chapter

Chapter 10

Draw your world

Now that you have a draft plan, you have one big decision left to make: what kind of advocate do you want to be?

The most important thing that will define you as an advocate is where you place yourself in your advocacy world. On the lines below fill in the elements you will use on the map.

Your first name:

_____

Your cause:

_____

Your top 4 supporters (the people you will turn to for help):

_____   _____

_____   _____

The center space
Just as your campaign plan needs a clear goal, your advocacy world needs a center point. Whatever is at the center will influence all the other choices you will make along the way in your journey.

Take a moment to close your eyes and try to visualize success. What kind of images come to mind? Are you thinking about personal success like awards, recognition and advancement in your career? Or are you thinking about the success of your cause like the people helped, the results achieved and the benefits of a better world?

If you are thinking about personal success, write your name in the center space. If you are thinking about the success of your cause, write the cause in the center space.

Supporting spaces
Now fill in the remaining spaces with the names of your supporters and either your name or the name of your cause (whichever one you didn't write in the center). How your supporters think about their role will depend greatly on how they are positioned in relationship to you. Are they a fellow supporter with you working on behalf of the cause, or are you asking them to work on behalf of your own advancement?

My advocacy world

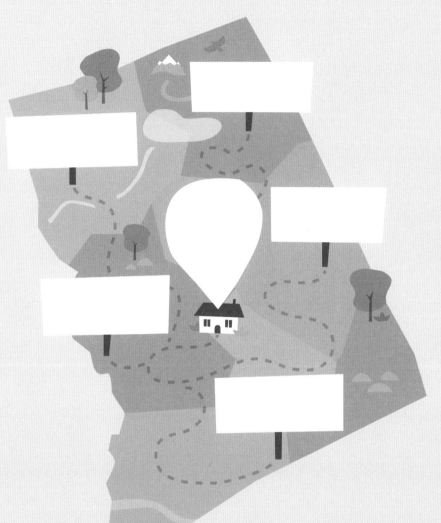

There is no right answer to how your draw your advocacy world. If you placed yourself at the center of your map, we hope you take the information in this book and use it to the best of your abilities to improve the world around you. If you put your cause at the center of your map, we would like to invite you to consider joining our community of advocates by turning the page.

My notes from this chapter

"A leader is best when people barely know he exists. When his work is done, his aim fulfilled, they will say: we did it ourselves."
—Lao Tzu, founder of Taoism

Chapter 11

The 50CAN community

Welcome to the 50CAN fam! 50CAN was created to provide a home base and a supportive community for advocates like you. We aim to be a place where talented people are able to do the best work of their lives in a culture that supports and sustains them. The glue that holds this community together is a team spirit grounded in our shared commitment to putting our cause at the center of our advocacy world.

Our P.O.R.C.H. values

What defines us as a community are the values we aim to uphold in our daily work.

Plussing it
Borrowing a phrase from Walt Disney, we challenge ourselves to do great work and then go a step beyond that...and then a step beyond that. We strive for "better" and "best" on behalf of our cause.

Optimism
We believe deeply in the American Dream and our ability to foster real change in our communities, even when faced with seemingly insurmountable odds. We approach tough challenges with high spirits.

Relentless
We are dogged in pursuit of our mission and our goals. We don't back down.

Candor
We are authentic about our challenges, mistakes and triumphs. We're honest with others and with ourselves.

Humility
We know we don't have all the answers and that we can only succeed by constantly testing our assumptions, working in deep collaboration with others and grounding ourselves in diverse viewpoints from across our states. We learn from our successes and our failures and strive to constantly improve.

Our work

We hope this guidebook is helpful to advocates working on a wide variety of causes. At 50CAN, we want to learn from and contribute to the work of as many citizen advocates as possible. The cause at the center of our work is education. We support individuals at the local level who advocate for a high-quality education for all kids, regardless of their address. We've built a team that provides citizen advocates with trusted research and proven tools so they can drive the creation of stronger, more equitable schools in every state and community in our country.

How can you join our community of education advocates?

Continue your journey online

Want to learn more about some of the tactics we use? Need extra templates and worksheets for your campaigns? Visit guidebook.50can.org for these resources and more. And check back often, as we'll be continuing to update the page with new tips and materials as our network grows.

Sign up for our emails

Want to learn more about what we are doing right now? Sign up for our emails at 50can.org so we can keep you plugged in to everything happening across our network.

Apply to a training program

We offer both full-time and part-time training programs and other opportunities for engagement across the country. Find out more about these programs and how to apply on the Programs page of our website.

Share your progress

Take a picture of your campaign plan and post it on social media using the hashtag #OpenAdvocacy. Then, text 50CAN to 52886 to sign up for our text action alerts!

Start the conversation

Sometimes the best place to start is with a conversation. We would love to hear from you and talk more about how we might be able to work together. Email us at partnerships@50can.org and we will respond with a way to take the next step.

Join a campaign

We aren't in all 50 states yet, but if we are in your state, we would love for you to get involved as a volunteer, intern, staff member or advisory board member. Visit the Careers page on our website to find out more about opportunities within our current campaigns.

Resources

Listening tour questionnaire

Who do you want to speak to?

Their phone number:

Their email address:

Their organization:

Their role at the organization:

Meeting date:

Prep questions:

→ Who do I know that knows this person?
→ What questions do I want this person to answer?
→ What is my main ask of this person?

After the meeting:

→ What follow up should I do now?
→ What asks did I make of this person?
→ What asks did this person make of me?

Listening tour questionnaire

Who do you want to speak to?

Their phone number:

Their email address:

Their organization:

Their role at the organization:

Meeting date:

Prep questions:

→   Who do I know that knows this person?
→   What questions do I want this person to answer?
→   What is my main ask of this person?

After the meeting:

→   What follow up should I do now?
→   What asks did I make of this person?
→   What asks did this person make of me?

The change lens checklist

Community

◯ Builds strong relationships with people served

◯ Draws upon a deep understanding of the local context

◯ Gives the community ownership of decisions

Competition

☐ Allows multiple providers to vie for users

☐ Provides high-quality information to users

☐ Gives providers incentives for improvement and success

Performance

◇ Empowers strong leaders to make decisions

◇ Sets rigorous standards for success

◇ Holds parties accountable for results

Pluralism

⬡ Allows for multiple, unique pathways to success

⬡ Encourages all groups to join

⬡ Embraces diversity and differences

The change lens checklist

Community

- ( ) Builds strong relationships with people served
- ( ) Draws upon a deep understanding of the local context
- ( ) Gives the community ownership of decisions

Competition

- [ ] Allows multiple providers to vie for users
- [ ] Provides high-quality information to users
- [ ] Gives providers incentives for improvement and success

Performance

- ◇ Empowers strong leaders to make decisions
- ◇ Sets rigorous standards for success
- ◇ Holds parties accountable for results

Pluralism

- ⬡ Allows for multiple, unique pathways to success
- ⬡ Encourages all groups to join
- ⬡ Embraces diversity and differences

The strategy checklist

Elite negotiation

- ⬭ An urgent public problem of interest to policymakers
- ⬭ Easily understood and credible options to act on
- ⬭ Incentives for legislators to make change

Social movements

- ◇ A clear call to action
- ◇ Compelling spokespeople who can dramatize the injustice
- ◇ Well-organized supporters and advocates

Expert communities

- ☐ A well-defined but complex public policy problem
- ☐ Expert agreement on the problem, causes and possible solutions
- ☐ Policymaker interest in expert guidance

Emergent networks

- ⬡ Well-defined areas of innovative practice related to the problem
- ⬡ Incentives for innovators to join together
- ⬡ Policymaker interest in translating practice into policy

The strategy checklist

Elite negotiation

○ An urgent public problem of interest to policymakers

○ Easily understood and credible options to act on

○ Incentives for legislators to make change

Social movements

◇ A clear call to action

◇ Compelling spokespeople who can dramatize the injustice

◇ Well-organized supporters and advocates

Expert communities

☐ A well-defined but complex public policy problem

☐ Expert agreement on the problem, causes and possible solutions

☐ Policymaker interest in expert guidance

Emergent networks

⬡ Well-defined areas of innovative practice related to the problem

⬡ Incentives for innovators to join together

⬡ Policymaker interest in translating practice into policy

Top tactics checklist

Elite negotiation

- ◯ Lobbying
- ◯ Power mapping
- ◯ Negotiation
- ◯ Policy analysis
- ◯ Bill drafting
- ◯ Coalition building
- ◯ Media relations
- ◯ Campaign donations

Expert communities

- ☐ Research studies and reports
- ☐ Legal action
- ☐ Conferences
- ☐ Public debates
- ☐ Advisory groups
- ☐ Policy proposals
- ☐ Letters to the editor
- ☐ Legislative testimony

Social movements

- ◇ Grassroots organizing
- ◇ Training spokespeople
- ◇ Marches
- ◇ Boycotts
- ◇ Sit-ins and occupations
- ◇ Storytelling
- ◇ Petition drives
- ◇ Door knocking

Emergent networks

- ⬡ Experimentation
- ⬡ Field visits
- ⬡ Peer networking
- ⬡ Toolkits
- ⬡ Newsletters
- ⬡ Trainings
- ⬡ Success stories
- ⬡ Social media campaigns

Top tactics checklist

Elite negotiation

- ◯ Lobbying
- ◯ Power mapping
- ◯ Negotiation
- ◯ Policy analysis
- ◯ Bill drafting
- ◯ Coalition building
- ◯ Media relations
- ◯ Campaign donations

Expert communities

- ☐ Research studies and reports
- ☐ Legal action
- ☐ Conferences
- ☐ Public debates
- ☐ Advisory groups
- ☐ Policy proposals
- ☐ Letters to the editor
- ☐ Legislative testimony

Social movements

- ◇ Grassroots organizing
- ◇ Training spokespeople
- ◇ Marches
- ◇ Boycotts
- ◇ Sit-ins and occupations
- ◇ Storytelling
- ◇ Petition drives
- ◇ Door knocking

Emergent networks

- ⬡ Experimentation
- ⬡ Field visits
- ⬡ Peer networking
- ⬡ Toolkits
- ⬡ Newsletters
- ⬡ Trainings
- ⬡ Success stories
- ⬡ Social media campaigns

Tell your story, one step at a time

Who do you know who is touched by this issue?

....

....

What needs to change?

....

....

Why does it need to happen now?

....

....

Pull it together into one short story below:

....

....

....

....

....

....

Now it's time to practice! Find opportunities to tell your story over and over again: in the car, in the shower, on a walk, to friends, to strangers, to anyone who will listen. The more you tell your story, the more effective at storytelling you will become.

Tell your story, one step at a time

Who do you know who is touched by this issue?

What needs to change?

Why does it need to happen now?

Pull it together into one short story below:

Now it's time to practice! Find opportunities to tell your story over and over again: in the car, in the shower, on a walk, to friends, to strangers, to anyone who will listen. The more you tell your story, the more effective at storytelling you will become.

Landscape analysis

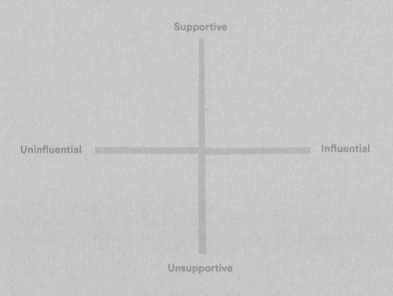

Supportive

Uninfluential

Influential

Unsupportive

Power map

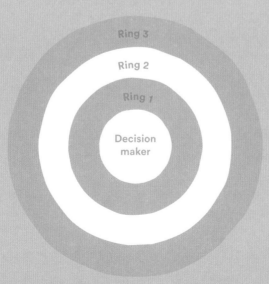

Ring 3

Ring 2

Ring 1

Decision maker

Landscape analysis

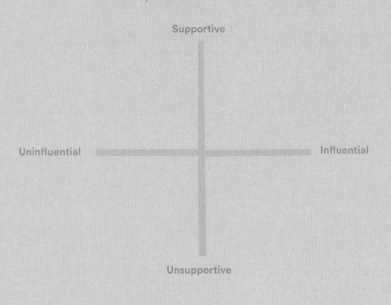

Supportive

Uninfluential   Influential

Unsupportive

Power map

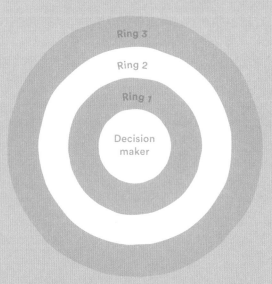

Ring 3

Ring 2

Ring 1

Decision
maker

Negotiation worksheet

Goal

A negotiated agreement must include...

Best alternative to a negotiated agreement (BATNA)

1.

2.

3.

Negotiation worksheet

Goal

A negotiated agreement must include...

Best alternative to a negotiated agreement (BATNA)

1.

2.

3.

My campaign plan

Goal

Strategy #1

Strategy #2

Tactics linked to strategy

1.
2.
3.

Tactics linked to strategy

1.
2.
3.

A win looks like:

Potential obstacles:

My campaign plan

Goal

Strategy #1

Strategy #2

Tactics linked to strategy

1.
2.
3.

Tactics linked to strategy

1.
2.
3.

A win looks like:

Potential obstacles:

My advocacy planner

January	February	March

April	May	June

July

August

September

October

November

December

My notes

Printed and bound in the USA by SOURCEALL MEDIA